A Form of Resistance

REASONS FOR KEEPING MEMENTOS

Luis García Montero
Translated by Katie King

For our wonderful friend Holly!

Love,
Katie

Doolittle Project Publishing
Seattle, Washington U.S.A.
All Rights Reserved
Originally published as *Una forma de resistencia*
©Luis García Montero 2012
English Translations, Introduction and Translator's Note
©Katie King 2013
ISBN-13: 9780692453735
ISBN-10: 0692453733
Print on Demand by CreateSpace
Cover design by Wendell Minor
http://minorart.com/
Author photo ©Katie King 2013
@ktking
Doolittleproject.wordpress.com

For Mauro, who is here,
though now he is leaving home.

Contents

Introduction

THE FIRST DECADE of the twenty-first century was a glorious time for Spain. At the dawn of the new millennium, it had shaken off the shroud of its reputation as a tragic country most famous for civil war, dictatorship, and repression. Democratic institutions consolidated, the economy grew, cultural activity flourished; even Spanish sports teams and stars couldn't lose in soccer, tennis, and Formula 1. Tourists flocked to Spain's gorgeous beaches and sophisticated cities. The country's cuisine was acknowledged as among the world's best; its wines, coveted. Sleek new highways and state-of-the-art high-speed rail connections zipped prosperous business executives and entrepreneurs as well as tourists around the country. Spaniards had jobs, many of them in the booming housing industry. They became homeowners, and owners of cars and electronics. Spain in the new century plunged into the first-world flush of spending on things.

And then that world collapsed.

The U.S. housing bubble burst and blew away the financial house of cards that mortgage banks had built to support it. It wasn't long before Spain felt the blast of the global banking crisis. In 2007, Spain's unemployment rate was 8 percent. By 2012, a quarter of all Spaniards were jobless and more than half of Spaniards under 25 were out of work. Almost a quarter of all families were living below the poverty line. Government austerity measures designed to control the deficit increased the suffering. Foreclosures skyrocketed and people lost their homes and their things. Hunger grew. Frustrated citizens protested in the streets.

It's a shocking turn of events that's difficult to understand, and it has stirred Spain's rich tradition of using interpretive poetry and prose to explore the meaning of what the nation is living through. Antonio Machado's poetry gave voice to the fears and uncertainties of a generation of Spaniards closing out the nineteenth century during the collapse of the Spanish Empire. Poets of the Spanish Civil War Federico García Lorca and Miguel Hernández ensured that the tragedy of that event was interpreted not just for Spaniards but for the whole world through their poetry and plays. And now the Granada-born poet Luis García Montero, who hails from the same Andalucian city as Lorca, is carrying on that tradition in the twenty-first century, with his poetry of realism capturing the human impact of larger world events.

One of Spain's most prolific and popular poets, García Montero has created in *A Form of Resistance* an ingenious and charming collection of essays – poetry-in-prose that explores the humanity in the little things we save and treasure and which give meaning to our daily lives. The book was inspired, García Montero says, when he reread John Steinbeck's *The Grapes of Wrath*, in which a farming family loses everything in the U.S. Great Depression. As Spain has spiraled into economic crisis, García Montero explores ways to resist and fight back by holding on to what is meaningful.

His writing is very personal. He writes about his armchair, his father's old cigarette pack, the mirrors in his home, a tie given to him by the poet Rafael Alberti. His mementos include a Zippo lighter, toy soldiers, a birthday card handwritten by his daughters. "Things are stories," he writes in his introduction. And stories connect humans to each other and to their past, and help them to understand their present.

García Montero is a poet of Spain's transition to democracy, when the nation lived at once in fear of the dying dictator and his supporters and in hope that democracy would flourish after he was gone. The decades after General Francisco Franco's death were difficult, tense, and uncertain. Political freedom was not a foregone conclusion. Change came slowly, with setbacks along the way. In the 1980s and 90s, García Montero spearheaded a style called Poetry of Experience, which featured everyday language and stories but reached deep for emotional connection. His work reflected the soul of a nation in transition. He won his first poetry award in 1982, the Premio Adonis for *The Foreign Garden*, and has since won both Spain's National Literature Prize in 1994 and the National Critics

Prize as well as the Lowe Foundation Prize. Today, he is a popular public figure who writes columns and op-ed pieces in the leading Spanish newspapers, is frequently called on as a public commentator, and has written lyrics for Spanish musical artists including Miguel Ríos, Joan Manuel Serrat, Joaquín Sabina, and Enrique Morente.

The Spanish experience seems to have universal appeal. The Spanish Civil War, a brutal dress rehearsal for World War II in Europe, inspired volunteers from around the world to join the fight to defend the beleaguered Republican government against Franco's army. The conflict also inspired extraordinary works of world-class literature that are today familiar to English-speakers everywhere.

Spain's current troubles also echo the world over, having their roots in a global financial crisis. The economic pain in Spain may be more acute than in North America and northern Europe, but the real hardship that millions of normal people are experiencing is the same. Luis García Montero's Poetry of Experience will ring true to those readers, and to all those who know and love Spain.

Katie King
London
February 2013

PROLOGUE

An Appreciation of Mementos

BANKERS COUNT THEIR profits, politicians count their votes, and poets count their mementos. They count and recount the things that are tangled up in their lives. In my days of meditation and solitude, of domestic vagabonding, I become aware that my house is full of objects. It's not that I'm bothered exactly by throwing things away, rather that I am inclined to keep the things that are my home. Don't throw the baby out with the bathwater. Be aware of what you lose when you toss your home away. Things that have the capacity to become memories represent your personal desire to participate in life, to live with attention, with love. "I pay close attention when I kiss you," wrote the poet Ángel González. Love has a bad reputation among inquisitors and literary tribunals; they condemn it to the dungeon of decency, soap operas, and sentimentality, because a lover, someone with the capacity to look intensely at another, is less docile, more dangerous than a professional conspirator. Lovers are paying close attention when they kiss, and those who live with close attention, with great love for life, often fill their homes with things.

Objects are the guardians of memory. Wiping the dust from your things, old objects now with new life, implies a loyalty, a struggle against mortality, a sentimental opposition to the deficiencies of the world. On the shelves of outlet stores, everything has its price. In the cupboards or on the bookshelves of your house, objects suggest an appreciation, a form of resistance against the rush of an irrevocable past. You pay for buying things and throwing them away, especially for throwing them away, an act that convinces us that the world is empty, that to exist is a permanent and insatiable exercise in devouring that emptiness. Into our garbage cans go the bottles, cans, cartons, plastics, the leavings of the banquet. Into the same garbage cans also go the days, the scenery, the cities of our childhood, the beaches, and the unfortunates who arrive in rickety rowboats along our coasts, swallowed up by the great containers of history. It's a human cost, as calculated as the earnings of the banker. "Passing by the bank, the banker said to me..." could be the opening lines of a new song. The price of things has to do with the insatiable hunger of an empty world. The appreciation of things speaks of a world that is full, with pain and with pride, where life counts, and where life attentively counts its things.

Things are stories, a brief course in philosophy, a form of caring. Life gets tangled up in things patiently waiting to be seen, and the will to live together provokes an intimate acquaintance, an amorous possession in which one ends up becoming the object of one's objects. Obsessions, delusions, ancient weaknesses, dates, and trips; everything lingers in things, which give testimony and guard memories both bitter and sweet. Things are objects with which we cohabitate, they know us and allow us to know ourselves; they form an intimate curriculum, a humane version of our criminal histories. Our misfortunes and our fortunes permeate our things. When the wires of our memories get crossed, it's convenient to have the help of things, their vigilant oversight. The years take their toll; they impose a way of understanding time that's helped by appreciating things, a heritage we can bestow upon ourselves.

The market fixes, like time, the price of things. We base our appreciation of this price on how we live and love. Our days are counted and our things are counted. The banker counts his profits and the politician his votes. On reflective Saturdays, with the great capacity for love innate only to loners, I need to count and recount my things. I don't waste time; I lose myself in time around my home. I recognize myself for what I am, without submitting myself to the immediate results of who I am. I tramp around the house and look at my schoolboy letter, my father's cigarette pack, my first long-play record, photographs of my youth, ID cards, the tri-color scarf, the Eiffel Tower souvenir from my first trip to Paris, Alberti's tie, inscriptions in books, old notebooks, the photos in which I feel like just another thing embraced by the past, childish drawings by my kids, my pacifist stickers from '86... Is it a museum? No, it's a landscape.

Chapter 1

The Glass

On waking one morning, after an uneasy sleep, Luis García Montero found himself on top of the dining-room table, transformed into a wine glass. Everyone expects and fears his own metamorphosis. He proved once again that in the prose of life, all comparisons are odious. He was rigid and damp like a watch dipped in water, firm as a soldier with no will, like a guard without eyes who sees everything out of habit, like a sky coated in clouds and lip smears, like a ghost-ship run aground among the dirty dishes, ashtrays, and napkins. Enough comparisons! Life rhymes, and conversations are what make existence perfect. What is happening to me? You drank too much again, he thought, and tried to wake himself from the dream, to break the cold shroud of the nightmare.

But he wasn't asleep. He was a glass, mute, paralyzed, inflexible, impassive. All objects are enclosed in themselves, their hearts strapped into straitjackets. Luis García Montero tried to move, stretch a leg, extend a hand, breathe, shrug, lie down, turn over, lean on his left elbow, show some sign of life, pinch himself, shout. Nothing. He remained still on the table, he was a simple abstraction, an immobile and exorbitant transparency. Lacking eyes, he saw everything around him; lacking ears, he heard motors out on the street, the loading and unloading of the day, his wife's breathing at the other end of the house and her slow stirring in sleep. The morning light brushed across his crystalline body, the confusing transparency of his skin, but left no trace of warmth in the vacuum. With the thirst of those who have already drunk it all, with the unsatisfying fullness of those at an endless feast, with the agitation of paralysis, he was there, immersed in the stillness of objects, incapable of desire, overwhelmed by need.

"Which glass am I?" he asked himself. Ah, I am the last glass, the only one left from my grandparents' crystal set. I brought it from Granada. And what am I doing like this? He struggled to remember his steps from the previous night, the obtuseness that left him on the threshold of metamorphosis. After saying goodnight to his guests, he picked up a book, sat in an easy chair in the living room and tried to relax, sip a whisky, read a bit while waiting for sleep to come. The conversation had left him uncomfortable, returning to a useless past. He needed tranquility. The past is lost, though not when it falls into a bottomless pit of time, but when it stops belonging to us or when we stop belonging to it. He thought this, and he rejected any feelings of guilt. You can't feel guilty for crimes you haven't committed. Of course not. The only clean glass was the one belonging to his grandparents. And that was it, done, the next morning he awoke as a glass among dirty glasses. He was round, fragile, hollow, and a breath of useless alcohol circled the calm awareness of his disorientation. The other objects observed him with the distant courtesy that recent arrivals provoke on interrupting a conversation.

The napkins, the ashtrays, the chairs, the throw on the sofa, the paintings, all began to talk of something else, politely changing the subject, to hide a secret, their secret, with the naturalness of little white lies. The things couldn't speak in front of him, because he was the topic of the conversation. A human being transformed into an object, a glass. He should win their trust. He needed to ask many questions. The language of objects has a vocabulary of silences, of looks, of absences, of habits. They live in the syntax of time, in the trembling grammar of latest fashions. Life passes them like a stream, and at times they fall into the current, float for a moment then disappear. Other times they remain like a song in the memory, like a chorus that returns to your lips when you least expect it.

Things can love their owners or lose respect for them, can keep a drunken conversation going with them. Luis García Montero tried to hum. He was about to start off a conversation with the things but they all suddenly fell quiet on hearing his wife's footsteps. She arrived clumsy, sleepy, unable to recognize him and with a tray in hand. She gathered up the plates, ashtrays, and cups. Please don't break me, don't break my grandparents' crystal wine glass, he thought as they walked toward the kitchen. She started the dishwasher. In Luis's head, there tumbled the intuition of a conversation silenced.

Chapter 2

Sweater

A SWEATER IS a domestic animal that summers inside the closet. But its vacation is full of spiritual exercises, because the closet is a familiar cave where you can learn the secrets of memory, shameful passions and vices. Sweaters are meant for the street, but in the closet next to the clothes they can inhale, better than in any other place, the silences that make up each thing's intimacy.

When autumn signs its cold-weather contracts, the sweater leaves the closet knitted with voluble shadows that we confuse with our own memories. Some clothes need a terrible stain, an amorous event, or the end of the day to separate themselves from our bodies. Some clothes depend on an accident of destiny, an inauguration, or a closing ceremony. Important affairs. But the sweater, ever since the invention of central heating, knows that its soul has become removable. You remove your sweater in the middle of a conversation, following the advice of humble climactic changes in a cafeteria or in a house. Like a domestic animal, with a spirit more canine than feline, the sweater allows itself to be draped over the arm of a sofa, on a chair, in any modest corner of daily life.

That which best defines us at first sight is what changes most, what moves most. Definitions are a pact with reality, a way of hiding transitory interests. We have become accustomed to everyday ethics in life. People take off and put on a sweater with the same naturalness with which they take on or shrug off a moral imperative. And that's how we live, moving between loves without surprises, decorating the desire to avoid pitfalls, to play politics, or to become a pencil-pusher. The resources of existence—rightly or wrongly, with humility or with ambition—mend the holes with the needle of necessity.

Among the archeological ruins of my closet, there sleeps a sweater of thick wool. It dominates the strata in which my infancy sacrificed its peace in the name of juvenile rebellion. When I was a boy, my mother, queen of family visits, liked to dress up her six sons in the same style of sweater. We formed a uniformed tribe, a textile staircase organized by age and height, which I no longer recall with the dismay of our flock, but with the melancholy of a broader world no longer nuanced by my innocent years. As I am the oldest, it was first up to me to dare wearing the distinctive knitted colors. In the middle of a school party, at the end of high school, I lit up a cigarette, took off my Sunday sweater and put on a Latin American hymn of thick wool, a loyal companion for attending avant-garde theater or concerts of protest music. A girlfriend gave me the sweater. I spent afternoons and evenings with her in students' apartments. This strange conspiracy that we call memory has decided that it remembers little of the scenes in which I took off my clothes with this old love, but it frequently recalls the hours that the sweater remained on the job, in the winter of the debate, distant from the reign of central heaters. A domestic animal, yes, but in a borrowed house.

Later, I left behind the naturalness of this rough sartorial adornment in search of a careful uncertainty, as though exercising my conscience, drawing boundaries to separate maturity and conformity, the sensible professor and the rebellious poet. And thus I knit my way along in the negotiations and choices of existence. Only those who truly know us should give us sweaters; prudence is required when meddling in others' futures. That sweater was so wide, so generous, that even today I can fit into it. The mirror, which is the only real enemy of the tricks of an everyday morality, murmurs that it doesn't look too bad.

CHAPTER 3

Armchair

YOU CAN GO far seated in an armchair. Walking is not the only way to forge a path; there are other ways to advance. Partisans of action seem to mistrust words, musings, any shift in thinking, so much so that at times they lose their way and walk in circles through the forest. But to act without rhyme or reason doesn't mean that what you see is what you get; rather, it allows you to be blown about by the wind, which is the way poets describe the fads and opinions inspired by advertising.

The ordinary is an untimely blast of wind that whistles across the houses and opinions of a citizenry disinclined to take note of their armchairs' nuances. Before walking, it's good to know where we want to go and which is the best road. That's why, as long as it isn't a justification for paralysis, sitting in an armchair is a way to advance by asking questions. Question marks are the armchairs of calligraphy; they are toboggans capable of providing diversion and velocity to seated bodies. There are answers, however, that tip us over like a bad run on the slope and we twist an ankle. My armchair is full of footprints, although I confess that this is not only due to the path that I forge seated here, but to the occasions when I use its belly and arms as a staircase. When I need to consult a book that sleeps in the clouds of the bookshelf and I don't have a stool to hand, I push the armchair across the room, I advance and I ascend thanks to its assistance. It is a spiritual elevation that does not separate my feet from the floor. The armchair—domestic geography for excellent afternoon snacks, late-night cocktails, and other affairs I shall not discuss—overcomes with experience any danger of excessive divinity.

I don't know if you can tell, but I love my tanned armchair with its dark brown leather. To it, I owe music, books, cities, seas, conversations and silences filled with unspoken words, resentments saved by sympathy, and injustices never committed. Armchairs don't ensure success, but they do help to avoid some foot-in-mouth moments, and they gift us the more productive side of solitude, which is also the most inoffensive. Instead of a pen, a watch, or a mobile phone, we should give our adolescent children an armchair. There is nothing more appropriate than an armchair for going out. Citizens who have their own armchairs don't have to cling to government seats, at the cost of starring in acts of disciplined humiliation or of false and vain rebellion. Those who know themselves to be the masters of their armchairs are struck with horror when they see so many upright and prosperous people obediently accepting atrocities ordered by a boss. They also feel a shy discomfort before the rebels who enjoy the disgrace of their old friends and align themselves with the opposing gang. They move so as not to change place. They protest. They swim to the other shore in order to continue participating under another disguise in the same spectacle. They cling to a government seat that they then upholster with stinginess rather than with a healthy conviction of independence.

I have never understood those travelers who go out into the world without leaving their armchair well prepared. It's like going to the doctor without changing your underwear. And it seems very dangerous to me that there are politicians who sit in a government seat without having in their homes an armchair to which they can return with dignity. It's important to pay attention to the place where one sits to read, a domestic frontier more necessary for human dignity than any international border. He who cannot claim his own private space is incapable of sincere emotion when in the public eye.

CHAPTER 4

Mirrors

THE MIRRORS IN my home can never agree when they talk about me. I pretend to be asleep, which is better than pretending to be stupid, and I listen to their comments, assertions, replies and counter-replies, charged with cruelty or comprehension depending on which side the shots are coming from. The mirrors' opinions are rescue flares; they sail through the hallways and sink into the liquid crystal conversations. On complicated days, when my deepest personal characteristics are on display, my house becomes a fireworks display, with thundering bursts of lightning that illuminate my political status, my religion, and the origins of my wardrobe.

My bedroom mirror is especially churlish. It doesn't like me at all; it can't abide my secrets, my obsessions, my smells, my baggy-eyed decrepitude, the way I dress to hang around the house. Maybe it sees me as I really am, in my wild-animal state, full of traitorous desires, carnivorous disloyalties, herbivorous fears, physical aches, bitter ambitions and unjust grudges. I am truly a spectacle in ripped slippers, too-short pajama bottoms and a prehistoric T-shirt. Though that is how the bedroom mirror sees me, truly this is not the full, real me; I feel guilty about my scruffiness, and I intend to amend my approach to undergarments and pajamas, and I feel very uncomfortable about my resentments and my coveting. The pink in my embarrassed cheeks is a permanent part of who I am. It is very embarrassing pretending to be asleep in my own bedroom.

The mirror in the entry hall has a different opinion about my character. It sees me leaving home somewhat more groomed. Though I'm not professionally elegant, the entry-hall mirror thinks that I make an effort to dress myself in an appealing manner, free from the middle-age weakness for adopting pathetically youthful airs but without falling into the premature aging of orderly people, too orderly, who sheathe their ideas in a blue suit and loafers. Also, the entry-hall mirror has seen me smile, greet visitors, receive idiots serenely, speak kindly to the disagreeable, praise bad books, compliment the beauty of plain people, tame my attacks of fury, and promise visits, reunions, and other special favors. Since it never observes my failures, the entry-hall mirror flares up its declaration that I am unselfish, generous, levelheaded, and cordial. I am grateful to it, but also embarrassed, and I try not to let it see the rosy hues that overpower my face, my ample face, when hypocrisy opens the way to solitude. Usually I race to the bathroom to splash cold water on my face.

The bathroom mirror is not as cruel as the perverse bedroom mirror, nor as partisan and optimistic as its colleague in the entry hall. It respects my efforts to groom and compose myself before I go out without abandoning who I really am. With no hypocrisy, because it makes no sense to go in the bathroom and come out dirty, the bathroom mirror helps me to tidy myself. It is concerned more with the tidying that connects me with others than with the identity that separates me from them. That is another way to understand the truth, in which I can be more than who I am because the free will of man—as natural as hunger or thirst—allows me to be who I want to be, who I am able to be.

Every day I am more convinced that the art of living consists of nurturing a positive conversation with the bathroom mirror. I've always been envious of women in a bar or restaurant who, without raising any suspicions, go together to the restroom.

CHAPTER 5

Pens

THEY HAVE THE souls of ants; they always disappear. I wonder if the pens in my house line up, march through the hallway and dive into obscurity through some secret hole: this causes an unbearable breach in my day-to-day tranquility. I buy them; I distribute them, some in the desk in my study, others by the phone, on the night table, in the kitchen. But when I want to write a letter, or take down a number, or underline a book, or make a shopping list, I waste half an hour looking for a pen. The man who runs the stationery shop thinks I am a maniac obsessed by pens. I take bags, packages, and boxes of them with the irritating regularity of a dripping faucet or a toilet that won't go to sleep. When I ask him for printer paper or envelopes or a printer cartridge and he notices I am prowling around my uncertainty about the order, understanding my shyness he smiles and asks, "So, Luis, do you need any pens today?" "Well OK, give me a package of the ones with the red caps." My "colors" strategy doesn't really work. Blue, black, red, green, they all disappear just the same, and even when one does come out of its ant's nest, it only complicates the situation when the color at hand doesn't correspond to the situation. It's not a good idea to write professional letters in red ink, or poems with green ink. Neruda always wrote with green ink, and because he was a man of immense personality all verses written in green sound like Neruda. Neither do I get good results with my pricing strategy. For a while, I thought that expensive pens would be more obedient than the cheap ones, and I gave them to myself or asked for them as birthday presents. But in the end, rich or poor, all pens have the souls of ants. You just end up with no pen plus the guilt of having lost a gift or wasted money.

I use ballpoint pens instead of fountain pens because it infuriates me less when I lose them. Disenchantment is impossible when we don't let ourselves become enchanted to begin with. In one of my desk drawers I keep a limited-edition Montblanc Virginia Woolf fountain pen that was given to me by Francisco Ayala. I have never used it; I don't dare take it out of the box or even separate it from its certificate of authenticity. I know that as soon as I try to write with it even once it will disappear just like all the fountain pens, like all the pens in my house. The only real paradise is the one in which you can never live.

This morning I was just about to justify my most recent purchases to my friend at the stationery store with a humanitarian alibi. "What's new? Well, I belong to an NGO that is dedicated to distributing pens to schools around the world." But I don't like to mess around with good causes, and sooner or later he would end up discovering the lie or would start telling all the neighbors my name is Mr. Pen-Without-Borders. He would be right, because when it comes to good causes you should focus first close to home, and I am the catastrophe of pens personified. Although sometimes I misplace my glasses, or my keys, books, briefcase, or wallet will give me a scare, the truth is that these have never become a domestic problem, not even metaphorically. But pens have, and that's why I suspect that their disappearance is not just due to my disorganization, but also to my ingenuousness or to my impertinence. It occurred to me this morning, when I wanted to write a letter to the Three Kings and I couldn't find a pen in the whole house. Since I was a boy I have believed that it is possible to write letters to the future, even to write the future with our own hands, which is a reckless thing to do. It's like toying with the devil; like giving too much importance to a telephone number scribbled on a newspaper, an address written on a napkin, verses noted in a book, stationery paper bathed in perfume, ink that predicts the future. The list of good intentions leads to a black hole. I don't know, but the pens in my house must have the souls of ants.

CHAPTER 6

Glasses

WHERE ARE MY glasses? Every time someone knocks at the door or the telephone rings, my glasses take advantage of the moment to lose themselves. I confess that the same thing happens to me with glasses as with pens; they never wait for me in the place that we leave off. I am reading, the doorbell rings, the messenger gives me the envelope, I go back to my armchair... the glasses are gone. They aren't on the table or on the bookshelf, nor the radiator cover in the hallway, nor the table in the entry hall. Becoming far-sighted is a question of time, and not just the years that go by and humiliate our pupils but also the hours that you have to spend finding your glasses.

The simple fact is that at a certain age truth becomes fuzzy if you come too close to it; it loses its edge, profile, sharpness, audacity, and you need to carefully seek out a corrected view, lenses that allow you to round out the meanings with your eyes. But that takes time, because the glasses get away or get smudged and you have to go to the kitchen in search of a few drops of dish soap; then the path back to the armchair is a dangerous expedition in which the imprisoned glasses find thousands of opportunities for escape. The glasses flee just as dogma, security, and authority flee. They prefer to give time a bit of time; they oblige you to seek out your own point of view, which should not be confused with the dazzling vision of absolute truths. Glasses are for the eyes of those who learn to be patient with age, not for the blindness of curmudgeons.

Those who cling to an inflexible self-identity forget that the world is alive because of its constant metamorphosis. Inside the shell is the sea, and the seas are moved by the will of the clouds, and the water in the clouds dreams of being soil, and the soil tries to ascend through the rings of the trees and the trees want to become the wind and they extend their branches to fly like a bird to the clouds, which will return the water to the sea and the sea to the shell.

It's only when you begin to lose your glasses that you dare to look inside yourself to see the rebellion that crouches within your routines, or the conservative spirit that hides inside some dissidents, or the child that runs through the hallways of maturity, or the parent that resides there in your eyes even though you pretend you don't look a thing like your own mother or father, or the women's tears that flow beneath the false rationalism of men, or the chill that stalks certain emotions. Glasses excite the secrets of the house because they are familiar with the labyrinth of metamorphosis.

I examine an awareness of lost time. It's an inventory of my footsteps. As far as I can tell, this morning my glasses turned into a cup of coffee, then they became a toothbrush, later in the afternoon they became the soul of the sofa cushions, then like seagulls on vacation they went to the blue tranquility of my forgotten folders in the office, they bared their claws like a cat wanting to play on the carpet in the library and they later transformed themselves into a pen before finally recovering their original condition of glasses. It must be unbearable to live twenty-four hours a day always in the same state of being, with the same robes or the same uniform. I am not able to read or write without glasses so I've had to wait for them and endure until they tired of wandering like spirits through the house. But I've already forgiven them. I can always take advantage of the time to think, and they give me the gift of perspective when I need to focus on reality.

CHAPTER 7

Shower

NEITHER HOT NOR cold, the water rains down at the perfect temperature, like the warm blue that illuminates spring mornings. The water cascades down, embracing and sheltering the skin, murmuring calming words in the ear, running its fine gentle fingers down the head, tangling the hair, traveling down the back with a firm meticulous caress, and little by little imposes a slow musical rhythm, music to dance to without moving, attending to the dampness of the lips, the surrendering of the shoulders, the controlled pelting on the chest, the timid trembling that skates down the belly, the groin, the thighs.

The water carries with it toward the drain the dirty memories of past hostilities and future uncertainties. It knows how to clean at once both the skin and the world around it, the traces of the night and the plazas veiled in pollution. You must be thankful because it doesn't always turn out like this. There are mornings when it is impossible to adjust the temperature; the taps are poisoned and disoriented, swiveling in a vicious circle from right to left, lurching from a wounding cold to the aggressive, suffocating heat of a domestic inferno. These indomitable drops that pound across your heart like a herd of wild horses can often cause associated accidents. I am familiar with the cruelty of a shampoo bottle falling with misery-making marksmanship on my big toe, or the pathos of the bathrobe that finally breaks the peg and lies agonizing on the floor, soaked through and useless. Not to mention those swampy slips and slides…

But this morning, there is none of that. Luck runs like water in my favor. My skin, heart, bathrobe, slippers, coffee machine, and blue sky are in their places. Historically, poets' moods were tied to landscapes and nature's seasons and were as sensitive as a young woman's awareness of an admiring look. When these poets suffered amorous catastrophes, the branches of the trees drooped their depression over the countryside and the cattle grazed listlessly on the grasses of grief. These days, domestic landscapes take the fore and organize themselves around the mysteries of the soul. Pantheism has been privatized and adapted to the dimensions of the home. The window-blinds, the clothes on the floor, the bathroom door, the mirror, and the water in the shower are all affairs of the soul.

The warm shower this morning falls on the nakedness of my first-person singular, on the "I" that forges ahead with life, hope, and serenity. All things breathe in their proper place, masking a tranquil soul. Under the liquid cape of water the first-person singular unites its essence and its existence in absolute complicity with its being. I am who I am. I don't need to feel any other way. I have no other need than to abandon myself to the sensations of the skin. It's enough for me to allow the water to carry away the old tensions, sudden irritations, emotional complexes, and accumulated bad times.

This morning God is temperance in the flesh, the shampoo keeps its balance, the bathrobe stays dry and ready on its peg, and the water embraces me and melts me like a lump of sugar in a cup of hot coffee. A good shower is just an advance on a good breakfast, a good greeting from the doorman, a good plaza, a good morning, a good blue in the spring sky, a good newspaper stand, good news...

It's a shame that God doesn't exist and that it's not sufficient to privatize His splendor with a good shower. The steps we take toward a precarious divinity can quickly lead us to a dump, which is the temple of all things broken in this world.

CHAPTER 8

Clothes

IT IS RIGHT and just that the mistress of your clothes is also the mistress of your nakedness. When I'm getting dressed to go out, I like to ask my wife to choose what I wear. That way I am coordinated, neat, and more or less presentable thanks to someone else's help, help that is also the care of complicity. The only really uncomfortable mask is the one you choose for yourself, the disguise that is an act of fear instead of an act of love.

The truth is that I don't know how to dress, but often my naiveté can give the appearance of a self-interested ruse. There is a rumor around my house that I have never learned to use the video player or to understand the laws of the technological jungle so that I don't have to be bothered with the procedures of daily life. Maybe this domestic gossip is accurate and my perplexity with electricity is due to a cautious indolence. But renouncing decisions about my dress is not a symptom of laziness. It is a pact between the disarray of my youth and the need to act like a grown-up.

As a characteristic, maturity defines us from head to toe. That's why I ask my wife to choose: hat or cap, jacket or sweater, dress slacks or jeans, shoes or boots? Learning the art of living is much like formulating a flexible balance between ideas and acts, private and public, dressed and undressed.

Of course my wife doesn't make it completely easy. "What look do you want for today? A poet or a professor?" That's her favorite question when she sees me heading toward the closet and the mirror after my shower. People assume that professors are respectable people, with a knotted tie for a heart and a leather briefcase for brains. And everyone knows poets are more bohemian, friends of a disarray that ranges from clean to provocative. But living long means you meet many crazy professors, calculating poets, and irresponsible bureaucrats who step into nonsense as often as a city official steps into his office.

It occurs to me that I'm more poetic when I dress as a professor, ready to discover some verse in the parsimony of a concierge. And I suffer attacks of civic respect when I go out dressed as a poet. The balances of a mature life are achieved through opposites. You grow when you have to resolve setbacks. It's no small thing to assume personal idiosyncrasies, to manage day-to-day sorcery as a testing ground for intimacy, dressing as a professor to inspire or as a poet to opine on issues of public education.

Logically the two things should live together, under control and with no rioting. Finding inspiration on the other side of the bed or on the other side of the moon should not be confused with finding points on the compass. Verse should not become a sermon. Lessons should not be emotional outpouring. You may feel like a foreigner in your own body, but your hat should still go on your head and your socks on your feet. It is about negotiating life with prudent restlessness. I think it was Juan Ramón Jiménez who said that of the two sisters, one always has something the other lacks. We can acknowledge and confess this without having to break with our own being.

When I come home and start to get undressed I learn a lot about myself, as much as when I dress in the morning. Depending on the day, the hat, the tie, the jacket, the suit trousers, and the black shoes end up in the most lyrical room, scattered and friendly like a few tranquil hours. In the room with the manuals and the teaching tools rest the cap, the sweater, the jeans, and the boots. The world is amusing thanks to functionaries who teach us to love poetry and poets who convince us that we need functionaries. And above all thanks to the true mistress of nakedness, who is the mistress of our clothes, in whichever room they may lie.

CHAPTER 9

Sandals

I TAKE THEM out of the suitcase from among the dirty clothes and I still don't know why I decided to keep them. I have to say again, my family doesn't understand why a spendthrift like me is so resistant to throwing things away. A pair of sandals torn when someone stepped on my foot should have ended up in the trash. It's not worth continuing the trip with them, bringing them home as if they were a gift. They'll end up in the corner of the closet, hidden among the shadows and useless objects, waiting for an eternally postponed trip to the cobbler.

I like holding on to used objects. They form a part of who I am; retaining my steps, my doubts, my scents, my haste, my lethargy, my cities. Cairo is a well-used city. It protects itself, but at a cost to the exuberance and vitality of its inhabitants, who are also its users. No one throws anything away there. Everything is usable, useful, used and reused, so that there is an accumulation of old cars, streets that smell of fearful pedestrians and gasoline, cafes with broken chairs, jackets with patches, tiny shops, tattered paper money, shouts, glances, feet stepped on, and a noble and ancient river that flows through the turmoil like a procession of wise men. Nothing stops here because everything comes from afar.

Walking through the street markets of Cairo with a broken sandal is a good way to mingle with life, a well-used life that leaves its mark on the vinyl in the car, in the burn holes in a shirt, scars on wood, sweat on the skin or on time, without trying to design or stylize its showcase. The city resists becoming a folkloric commodity, the picturesque version of the place most tourists expect. The vulgar way to distinguish between travelers and tourists is to group them: individuals on adventures through difficult lands or those who travel in flocks on programmed itineraries. But there is a distinction, and it affects your ability to see. Tourists see an abstract, a vignette, a schematic summary, a pre-established version of reality. Tourists look at reality to follow a map. Travelers look at maps to follow reality. They feel the footsteps, the bitter stink of life. In fact, you don't even need to leave your house to live as a tourist or a traveler.

Tourists take fright at this market whirlwind that smells of kebab. They fret at the bustle of djellaba robes, mosques, prayers, and cries that add up to the proclamation of the bizarre. I fret about the pride with which the women wield the indignity of their scarves, their resignation and their identity. Tourists make an effort to overcome the uncomfortable presence of filth, the smell of used things and the traces that the different races, religions, and poverty leave on your hands. There are traces in eyes, robes, clothes, utensils, and breath. They are the traces of reality.

I know many people from Granada who are fearful of the crowded Calderería Vieja, the Arabic section of our city, even though they feel great pride for the tenth-century Arabic-built Alhambra, which they feel is part of their own history and cultural heritage. I've seen many tourists flee from the dirty sandals of the Cairo street markets while later gaping in admiration of Tutankhamen's sandals. It's not just about bad smells. They are bothered by the details of a particular kind of experience, of flesh-and-blood stories. For them, Tutankhamen represents Man and Humanity, the place of everything, the treasure that makes us proud. But you have to erase so many used things, so many smells, so many impressions, so many centuries, in order to arrive at Tutankhamen's sandals, that we run the risk of leaving ourselves out of place, of living in our homes as tourists without discovering the essences of ourselves in the vocabulary of objects.

We need to find a point of agreement between the nothingness of the pharaohs and the excessive carnality of repression. I brought my broken sandals back in my suitcase, just in case one day they tell me something about what I learned in the street markets of Cairo.

CHAPTER 10

Clocks

THE CLOCK IN my kitchen is eight minutes slow, but nobody is fooled. It knows that I know that time runs through its hands eight minutes late, so there's no malice in what it says. When I see the hands showing ten minutes to eight in the morning, I know I have two minutes to finish breakfast so I can leave the house at 8 a.m. on the dot to get my daughter to school. Time should be objective, but instead it's filled with private blunders strapped to your wrist and hanging from your wall.

We only survive this with a measure of dignity because public time is a collective river in which private blunders learn to float on private solutions like wood, paper boats, or plastic balls. In my kitchen, I launch a paper boat filled with eight extra minutes. Thus, I deliver my daughter on time to her school. It's not a trick; it's a family pact, an understanding. I don't bother setting the clock to the correct time because I understand that the clock is not trying to fool me with its lateness.

Some friends manage their relationships to time by deploying innocent tricks. Those who are always late set their clocks an hour fast to battle their tendency to be tardy. The more nervous among my friends protect themselves against being too early by setting back the minutes and the appointments on their watches. These adjustments and corrections serve to keep us from bursting the seams of time or from allowing it to become too loose. But the kitchen clock isn't slow because of a trick; it's slow because I recently changed its batteries. I made a mistake as I was resetting the time; I discovered the paper boat filled with eight minutes and I got used to its navigation without danger of shipwreck.

Personal tricks I reserve for my alarm clock. It's pleasing to know that it is fast. I listen to the first headlines of the day at 7:15 and remember that actually it is only 7 a.m. The future takes measure of that quarter of an hour, fifteen minutes of dozing, warm sheets, and laziness. It's not that I want to fool the alarm clock, because I know that it knows that it's only 7 a.m. and I'm not going to get up until 7:15. Sprinting toward the future isn't terribly dangerous if you only try to take advantage of a bit more of the present, to adjust your emotions with reality. This is what writers do; they travel to the past or the future in an effort to find a good fit with the agenda in the present.

Elegies delay things, hymns advance them, but no one is fooled because fiction respects the wisdom of the present. Whether it's due to changing the batteries or a personal trick, moveable time in fiction doesn't impede coexistence. You know it's midnight, even if the clock strikes seven in the morning. You can use the light of an imagined sunrise to illuminate the darkness of a real nighttime. The danger comes when the clocks jump ahead or fall back convinced that the hour is accurate, the hands on the clock face promising perfect time. If this happens the clocks become, more than fiction, counterfeit, a rosary of superstitions. They land us in places that aren't yet open or have already closed. This has happened to me on occasion with my wristwatch, a good and perfect gift, so sure of its engineering that it is capable of convincing me of anything. If it errs, I err along with it. As much as poets might say otherwise, time stumbles, yes, it stumbles, and often on that same rug or that same curb. It stumbles especially when it becomes history and rolls along with the pride of perfect engineering. That's when it sees with the eyes of a priest or an economist.

Chapter 11

Refrigerator

THE REFRIGERATOR IN my house is an electro-domestic adolescent. I suppose that electro-domestic appliances, like dogs and nudes, look like their owners. Observing the character of the dog can help you understand the atmosphere of the house; it might be quiet or it might bite or bark or cower or jump up and wag its tail at visitors.

For many people, a dog is man's best friend. In my house, I have a cat called Negrín, because since I was a child life has led me across rooftops and toward freedom. Dogs only remind me of how in some houses I am a fleeting guest, a cautious being always wanting to move on. The same thing happens when I go to the beach. I cannot detach myself from an unshakable spirit of observation that distances me from any participatory instincts. A walk on the beach gives you a glimpse into the state of the world through the bodies you see there; the fine line between happiness and tragedy, elegance and horror, purity and contamination. Beaches and dogs help you to understand their owners, just like appliances, whose pulses mirror that of the hand that pushes their buttons or opens their doors.

Clearly a character is a bundle containing many twigs, and owners scatter the nuances of their personalities around the house. Appliances become living reflections of the owner's soul: weak-willed washing machines, dogmatic ovens, bungling dishwashers, strict juicers, modest vacuums, cynical microwaves, and adolescent refrigerators. The refrigerator in my house is an electro-domestic adolescent because it abandons itself to the excesses of its soul, divided between fullness of the heart and the wretched abyss of melancholy. There is no middle ground. It shifts from the perception of nothingness to the plenitude of a feast, from fervor for the world to a cold, pallid sky, undefined, like a frozen pizza.

Relations with the refrigerator are both sentimental and quotidian. The regulatory discipline of those who don't take chances with emptiness, expiration dates, a lack of ice at midnight, or an excess of optimism that ends up in the garbage, can have admirable results. An organized life can rescue a refrigerator from unwelcome inadequacies and waste. My refrigerator, which is the most adolescent of my appliances, is erratic. Its solitudes and excesses share a feeling of guilt. Instead of changing its ways, it ends up abandoning itself to the ups and downs of the pendulum swing. I see it move from cat-like solitude to the shared music of a party.

Yesterday, my refrigerator suffered a solitary but healthy affliction; it harbored only a yogurt, an alcohol-free beer, a can of pâté and a half-full ice cube tray. It was a bleak sight, the reflection of a prince in ruins, so I decided to throw a party. A shopping list is the best deterrent, the most convincing way to respond. Now, the refrigerator is packed and I can barely fit in the orange juice for Benjamín and María (they recently started drinking vodka with orange juice). There is tonic water for gin and tonics for Almudena and Juan, Coke for the rum and Coke for Chus and María José, and lots of ice for the whiskeys for Joaquín, Jimena, Regina, Miguel, Silvia, Felipe, Ángeles, Bienve, Javier, Rosana, and Ramón. EAnd wine and beer for everyone and alcohol-free beer for Conchita and Celia. There is meat for the barbeque, ice cream for dessert and even skim milk for Mariano, who will surely stay the night. I'm going to call them now, as my adolescent refrigerator advises.

CHAPTER 12

The Record

So it is: mementos connect us to the future. Only memory has the capacity to make itself felt in our present and influence our future. While we keep one eye on our history, we can keep the other alert and focused on our destiny. Reviewing what is past justifies what lies ahead: that which defines us and calls to us from a time we have yet to live. The most dangerous ghosts don't live in castles of the past. They live in the intemperate climate of a tomorrow without a yesterday, of a future we are condemned to live without memory. Remembering is like tying up your shoelaces at the start of a journey, and every day, no matter how old you are, is a journey.

The fetishes of memory are the only substantial company we can find on the empty pages of the mornings, with that vertigo felt by those of us who awake, arise, dress, and need to have a life ahead of us. I've always admired people who know how to die of old age in their beds with their whole lives in view before them. Optimism is sustained through loyalty to the past. Memories of home equip us with calm to join the community.

I've saved the first record I ever bought. It is also the first thing of my own that I ever bought. Sweets and toys belong to our childhoods more than to us. They are the legacy of our parents, an inherited happiness. I don't deny the value of childhood, but its impact can only be measured as it evolves us into the fractious selves we become. I began to become myself in some books and in the month of December, one afternoon when by good fortune my grandparents arrived for my ninth birthday party without a present. They solved the problem with some happiness made of metal, and the next morning I bought myself a record by Joan Manuel Serrat. It wasn't just the whim of a quirky kid.

My mother was a big fan of Julio Iglesias and my father was a decided defender of Raphael, so I, caught between the two, found an escape route in this Catalan singer-songwriter who had put music to the verses of a poet from Seville. I had heard the record in a literature class taught by a professor who understood how to compensate me for the many hours of cold and the monotony of rain against the windows. Our destinies sometimes turn on casual decisions made by others.

I kept the record, just as I kept the image of the schoolboy who had heard of the poet Antonio Machado and wanted to listen to his "Cantares" and his "Saeta" in the voice of Serrat. Sometimes objects make manifest that which is inside us. From the moment I heard that record, I began making myself into who I am; with happiness that is mine, with pain I call my own, creating the legacy of my own feelings, like an attack of doubt or a roll of the dice that doesn't eliminate chance but skips over it so that all ends well and with the right numbers up. Underlying my most sensible opinions there hides a young man who knows how to run better than the police and who learned to live to the rhythm of a guitar and a few true words. We should never lose respect for the adolescent we once were, nor laugh too hard at his utopian activism.

Lucidity should not become betrayal; it is, perhaps, the search for a new home for our passions, like a nice condo with an elevator, furniture, central heating, lots of amenities, and some select souvenirs. One day I was in my home writing, more mired than ever in the impure desires of my existence, when the phone rang. It was Joan Manuel Serrat. He had put music to one of my poems. He wanted me to listen to it and help write the chorus. The burst of vanity, understandable in the poet who hears his own verse in the voice of Serrat, quickly dissolved into a stronger emotion, into the image of a boy spending his first money on a record and the vivid feeling of an adolescent who joined life thanks to a few true songs. We must be loyal to the memories that tie us to the future. Memory is more like a musical score than an attic.

CHAPTER 13

Goya

SOME OBJECTS HAVE a special glue that traps life inside of them. These objects dwell in silence, discreet amidst the clutter of the bookshelves. There they are for years, accumulated without any specific motive, as if they had fallen asleep just outside the flow of appearances and disappearances that marks the rhythm of existence. They preserve the fingerprints of time, fingerprints on the water, and then one day they begin to speak the names of the past. They are the spokesmen of an era, of a style of dress, of visiting certain restaurants, of work, of meeting up with friends, or preparing for trips.

Last night I found, camouflaged between a Latin dictionary and a literature textbook, a pack of Goya cigarettes. My father smoked Goya many years ago, when the aroma of tobacco was not the disagreeable consequence of a vice but an atmosphere that often enveloped respectable people and children who did their homework at the dining-room table. I'm not aware of having consciously wanted to save that pack of cigarettes. It wasn't a milestone, a charm, or the symbol of a decision. But now it has emerged from the very core of my life, breaking its silence and blabbering like a chatterbox seen through the tinted lens of objects that get mixed up with memories. The Goya pack speaks of my father, of my errands to the tobacco store in Granada, and then winds itself up and launches into a theory about Spanish society during my adolescence. This was a time when people had begun cutting out of the cover of the cigarette pack the oval portrait of the Spanish painter Francisco Goya and using it to cover bottles and jars. Thus the humbleness of daily life was covered up, just as children's books are covered.

The jars carefully adorned with the round and genial face of Goya walked the fine line between Spanishness and honest insecurity. In my memory I associate them with the cars dressed for Sunday in crocheted seat pads and nodding dogs on the dashboard. Families showed off their new shoes for Corpus Christi, dressed in new clothes to go to the doctor, and preserved the cheap delicacy of their coffee sets in glass cupboards where guests could see them. China coffee cups, porcelain figurines, a whim of crystal, were luxuries in a country without luxuries, and the expression of courtesy among the poor. Manual laborers, men forced to work as handymen, and industrious housewives also belonged to a reality that required them to make the most of their situation without much chance of success.

More than money itself, what counted then were the gestures in a life that was poor but decent; scrubbed and combed, we were respectful in our greetings and smiled when standing to give up a seat on the bus. The Goya-covered jars reflected something more than gaudy taste. They facilitated a momentary union of the filigreed and the industrious sides of families who had not yet been invited in to consumerism. Their aspirations for social improvement left the displayed coffee sets at home and went out on the streets in the form of nodding dogs and seat cushions. It wouldn't be long before fear went out into the streets too, and freedom without ire, and savings accounts.

We were prepared to cover up the illusion of democracy. Many people covered it up like a Goya jar or a shop window on Main Street. Although I don't believe that tackiness was the worst sin of the Transition.

CHAPTER 14

Chairs

THE CHAIRS HAVE been crazed all through the holidays. Their comings and goings around the house reflect our need to find a place in the world, and the trials of spirit and space that arise when we want to accommodate everyone. Though hermits hate to hear it, we are all wedded to the world, to everyone in the world, in life and in death, in intelligence and in stupidity, and that's why the chairs go back and forth from the kitchen to the living room, from the bedrooms to the dining room, from the final drops of late-night champagne to the books piled on my desk.

Chairs everywhere and in every condition: they symbolize celebration and community when they gather together in their various motley styles around the dinner table, or they become the memory of loneliness if they appear in a dark corner of the house, the garage, or the bathroom. The good thing about a chair is that you can move it. Over there someone went off to enjoy a moment of respite from the tumult between the happy arrival and the happy departure. Over here the domestic multitudes gathered to renew their conversations.

Chairs are always chasing an ashtray, a drink, or a guitar. They are an atlas of human geography with various heights and colors, jammed in together around tables, matching the metallic cold of the kitchen, the casual atmosphere of children's bedrooms, the elegant wood of the library, and the broken uniformity of the dining room that has been overwhelmed by the party, the hustle and bustle of family reunions or of nights drinking with friends. To many people, sorrow seems more respectable and spiritual. There are those who favor guilt, pain, seclusion, and death. I prefer the punishment of listening to a Christmas carol, even after the tenth time at the table of some distant cousins, to the drum of

Easter Week. I spend all my time trying to find chairs for others, but I wouldn't wish a cross on anyone.

The holiday is as inhuman as a tragedy, but less unjust. Not even when people confuse happiness with consumerism—the hedonistic stupidity of the commercial society—do I doubt the advantages of joy that is shared with others and of carefully chosen gifts. Faced with the threat of a penitent enamored of pain, I prefer to suffer the sharp-elbowed shopper on the first day of holiday sales or a relative who repeats his toast every five minutes at an ever-increasing volume. Of all the kinds of avarice, a sordid desire for pain is the one that truly seems to me a lie. More than a lifestyle that consecrates death, what is admirable are those people who love life and join in solidarity in the face of pain and death. These are the people who reign over the kingdom of the chairs that gather together, mixing their different races, around a bottle of whiskey, a conversation, and various complicated songs, until the rooster crows.

I have a weakness for the chair where people dump their coats. Keeping its distance, it observes a proper silence like the old lighthouse-keeper who lives in solitude to assist the navigation of the party. People arrive and take off their coats, their wraps, their various forms of fighting the cold outside. Throughout the night, the coat-chair occupies its discreet position. It is vigilant, listening, playing music. Later it depopulates, indicating the point of farewells. That's when it begins to take on the air of an empty box, broken toys, Christmas decorations returned to the closet, an outdoor party ruined by rain as summer ends. The coat-chair is where the melancholy can sit for a bit just before heading off in search of a well-earned rest.

CHAPTER 15

The Space Heater

WHEN SPRING TAKES over in the garden and house, the space heater lives its autumn and acquires the melancholy air of a skeletal tree. It's out of place, like a bathing suit in the winter-clothes cupboard. It observes the sunlight in the house with the clumsy haste of one who has just been abandoned by the love of his life, or the pointless urgency of a clerk who has reached retirement age. Within its metallic fibers, the pulse of heat and amenability continues to beat, but there is no job it can do to justify this, the routine of its service, the reason for its vigilance. The house has forgotten it, or is in the process of forgetting, while the closets shift the order of the clothes inside them, the windows watch the last surprises of bad weather go by, and the floors receive their first greetings of bare feet.

The space heater doesn't protest. It is the most stoic invention of human prudence. It's accustomed to shifting from cold to hot, or from hot to cold, and it patiently dedicates itself to a task in which the endings and the farewells are just a prelude to the return. It is ignorant of the jealousies felt by the older brother when dethroned by the younger or the ire of a possessive lover or the rancor of a politician who loses an election and refuses to engage with reality so that the days and the months cannot live without him.

The only thing that really matters is that which can carry on without us and then end up coming back to us. Time dissolves and we know that although centuries have passed, everything happened yesterday. The space heater knows this. It has the soul of an elder grizzled by the things that come and go, like winter, love, everything that is true beyond fleeting ambition. It's prudent to mistrust things that must be impaled upon our talons in order to belong to us. Winter will return just as spring has returned and will be ours as we will also belong to it. That's enough waiting for a new year, enough waiting to turn the corner and surprise ourselves to find we are on a rainy Saturday looking into April.

The space heater knows Granada's secrets better than anyone. Though it lives under the warm mythology of Spain's south, Granada suffers harsh winters. The cold doesn't surrender to romanticized precepts. A tradition of building homes unprepared for the frigid temperatures has made space heaters, and the blanketed tables they fit into, familiar company. Granada is the kingdom of space heaters tucked into blanketed tables and of softly spoken desires. Cities that murmur their desires tend to shout out their secrets and throw them from the window.

Cold and news pass through the poorly shut windows and start to sound like street noise. A bad day in April is like a noise, like news stained with the coffee of rancor or speculation. It is a shudder that leaves winter's truck disappearing into the numbers of the almanac. In the kingdom of trucks, news and shoddy windows, the space heater is never just a childhood memory, even in the age of central heating. It is a central object in the household, the merciful heart of the cruelest months.

I knew that I was truly independent when I found myself in a store buying my first Granadian space heater. I have it here. It's come with me through each move, changing its age, its habits, and its city. In Madrid, I don't really need it but I know it needs me. I turn it on especially when spring nibbles at the edge of winter. I want the heater to know I haven't forgotten its company. And I observe the dignity with which, little by little, it says farewell to its service, its prestige in the family, the opportunity for its sermons—all without reproach, without raising its voice. I like space heaters when they have lost control of the legs under the blanketed table. Dignity is found not in beginnings but in endings.

CHAPTER 16

Notebooks

A BLANK NOTEBOOK isn't empty, it's an invitation to the future. Writing, like the law, brings order to reality through the power invested in it by imagination. Imagination is the eye at the keyhole through which we peek at ourselves. Our stories, dreams, desires, and experiences live inside our skin and inspire us to wander. They are temptations disguised as travel guides.

A blank sheet of paper is like a map of abstractions, full of who we are, what we remember, what we have done, what has been done to us, and what is circling in our heads. It seeks the tools with which to emerge in the form of words, which is how our hopes and fears find their voices. Hopes and fears are a response to the restlessness that resides in a blank sheet of paper or an empty notebook. I'm not convinced by innovators who turn words into a rational abstraction, erasing the past experiences that determine our identities. To make sense of the affirmation that we are all equal before the law, we have to begin by understanding that we are not all equal before history.

Nor am I convinced by the traditionalists who deny the capacity for invention and the promise of the future that blank pages offer. They believe only in the perpetual repetition of what has always been written the same way. It's good to use our imaginations to elaborate our identities, to make sense of living together, but that should not be confused with a torturous accumulation of splinters and fragments. The total is fortunately somewhat more than the sum of its parts. The total is a plot, a story that can be written in a blank notebook, a notebook that is not empty because in this blankness resides the erasure of an inheritance that observes us.

I have a weakness for notebooks. Thanks to notebooks our house is filled with journeys, because I navigate with them, because I like to buy them in far-off cities, or because the blank pages are like an itinerary, an airport lounge. Notebooks set the sails of a ship on the table, so that the wind can write its story while the sea opens and closes. I log in my notebook the address of the city hall where my friends are getting married and the starting time of a seminar on international relations and world hunger.

We are living in an era of navigation, good winds and notebooks to write in. Spain is prosecuting violence against women and stamping out prejudice and has legalized gay marriage. We are starting to realize that we are all equal before the law, but that we are not equal before history, and it's important to differentiate between the two. Spanish society is full of blank notebooks, stories, pages that remain to be written that aren't empty, rational reasons to feel proud of the ongoing essay that is life. But black ink stains the fingers of a world that is still accustomed to coexisting with misery. The economy has become a religion that sanctifies the avarice of the speculators, the suffering of the victims, and the general indifference of some citizens who don't feel that the problems of others are their own. It seems as though we have uncoupled civil rights and collective responsibility. My friends Carlos and Eduardo are getting married. A child dies of hunger somewhere in the world every six minutes. Isn't it possible to have individual freedom and global responsibility? Can we not fill the word 'respect' with social consciousness?

When the pirates of reality abandon us on an island, we must make sure to tuck away in our jackets our pens and blank notebooks. At times, they help us more than a book. We must look to the horizon and, in the shade of a palm tree, write whatever occurs to us, whatever lives within us, whatever is peeking at us through the keyhole of imagination. Write, for example, that the day is calm with the sun sparkling on the silvery spume of the waves and over the blue sea there appears the silhouette of a ship. The sails and the pages are coming to rescue us—the sails and the pages of a new composition.

CHAPTER 17

Alarm Clock

THE WORD 'DAWN' is very unreliable. If we open the door and just dash outside, anything can happen. The symbolism of dawn has become vain, with its mixture of solemnity and hypocrisy that makes it feel right at home whenever someone trots out a prayer or a patriotic song. Sung in chorus, there are dawns that turn the squares into bars full of drunks. They are a call for darkness to rain down.

Those who favor compromise in this life should seek out a different word, a term that puts things in their proper place. We live in a world that only allows optimism as a moral attitude, a daily grind without a glimmer of intelligence, a celebration of dogmatic faith. We must protect ourselves from perversity in the pleasure of sunrise, from the political exaltations of the aurora, the clichés wrapped in dawn, of cynical defeatism in the darkness of early morning. We need a pact with life that moves words to actions and allows us to keep working, pestering, and opining in the real world.

I am increasingly in favor of the alarm clock. It isn't prestigious in a world sickly-sweet with patriotic hymns, but it watches over my dreams with persistent dedication through the passing of time. There it is on the night table with its discreetly blinking red numbers. It is a pending bill as well as a moral concept. My alarm clock is not a rose, or a dove, or a donkey so soft it seems made of cotton, or a flag waving in the wind, or a pearly white smile. It is an artifice. An artifice too can assume symbolism beyond its own identity and what is sanctified in nature. My alarm clock is black, with a button for the alarm, a dial for the radio, and an obligation to make dreams compatible with work schedules.

The alarm clock has locked within its dispensary a mass of dawns, rays of light, and horizons. But it doesn't allow itself to be fooled by appearances. It brings clarity to daily life. Its future is not a bucolic promise or a perfect place. Its daily duty is to search for the hours and the minutes. In the dawns of the alarm clock, there are no patriotic hymns. All the space is taken up by the exhausted and hungover need to abandon the sheets and step forward. Alarm clocks bring us close to the blindness of the victor, but even closer to the sickly eyes of the survivors; to the intimate decision to leave the bed and strike up a conversation with the day, to the news of the world, to work and to sorrow.

Those who can ignore the time of night don't need an alarm clock. But good intentions are as fragile as paradise, they are full of edges and imperfections and even those of us who want to get to bed early are condemned to tardiness. The alarm clock is an essential device for those who decide to live in the moment, in the shadows of existence without relinquishing that last drink; for those characters who spring from obscurity like the confession of a friend. It's worth remembering as well that alarm clocks have long had a human dimension frequently used in literature at moments of great joy. The alarm clock is the watchman who announces an arrival: of dawn, of the father, of the husband. The alarm clock is the kiss that brings you to life in the middle of the night to make love. The alarm clock is the maestro who invites you to open your eyes and discover the folds of reality. The alarm clock is that which rouses our sentiments and unlocks our senses.

Chapter 18

Thinkers

I COLLECT THINKERS. A Peruvian peasant in Cuzco gave me an Incan Thinker that he had just dug up from his orchard, and ever since then I have purchased Thinkers as mementos of my trips. I display them in my living room, on top of the cupboard and the TV cabinet, all together, but each one on its own. Or at least that's what I thought.

Thinkers should be alone. With their heads in their hands, with their eyes concentrating on their souls or lost in the fog of infinity, with their taciturn melancholy awaiting an idea or the intuited arrival of love, the Thinkers abandon themselves to a discreet and mysterious preoccupation. They are dressed as African tribal chiefs, Chinese miniaturists, and sailors on a rainy day, young romantic lovers in the twilight or beautiful nudes bearing the overwhelming weight of their ideals and wisdom. Nudity is a convincing costume for living in a museum or in a collection of Thinkers.

There are incalculable ways of representing thought. In the most far-flung shop window when you least expect it you spot a skull with intellectual airs or a pensive frog or a revolutionary leader in the supreme moment of deciding his orders, or a thoughtful monkey or a reasoning demon or a bored angel passing eternity resting his hand on his cheek.

I had the impression that each Thinker, immersed in its musings, was reflecting on its own identity. When my Greek wise man fell to the floor, I glued his broken head together with great care. I didn't want to interfere with his determination to discover universal ideas that could provide us with the perfect abstract of the world. The mission of a collector is to avoid competing with any of his pieces, although sometimes he might be tempted to deny their importance.

The Greek Thinker's broken head was a casualty. It would have been unfair to compete with this romantic voyager, poised at the abyss of his internal rupture and tragically thoughtful upon discovering that reality, splintered and fleeting, is not abstract nor perfect nor sacred.

I assumed that the Incan Thinker thought about being Incan, and the Roman Thinker meditated on the divine origins of the Empire, and the Saharan herdsman delved into the desert spirit of the sand dunes, and the young student mentally balanced the vertigo of modern realism and instincts of permanence. But a few days ago I began to suspect that they are all thinking about me, that they are watching me and amusing each other with moral evaluations of my behavior. They are more concerned with my way of acting than their way of being.

Some clear evidence allows me to conclude that the porcelain Thinker from Galicia doesn't take its eyes off of me when I get home, checking to see if I have come home tired from work or, more likely, bumbling from imbibing too much alcohol. An English lady, an escapee from some royal palace, reviews my manners as I eat a sandwich while watching some talking heads discuss politics on TV. Maybe it's my fault for having brought them together, placing them all there together in the living room in an effort to give them order and meaning, relieving them of their solitude. But now they seem preoccupied with my habits, with how I dress and how I undress, with the books that I read, with the moments I act the fool and those when I am the wise man, with my phone conversations, with the way I file my bills, my receipts, my poems.

A strange passion for urbanity has filtered through the Thinkers in my collection. Gathered from distant eras, countries, and cultures, little by little they have reached an agreement to observe me. As I've said, they are less and less interested in their own way of being and more and more concerned with my way of acting at home. They are the ones who criticize me when I leave the lights on or when I turn up the music too loud. We will need to negotiate a pact between their being and my acting, or their acting and my being, in some neutral zone where their old ideals, previously so isolated, previously so devoted to entelechies and abstractions, can't turn into a neighborhood coffee klatch. By fleeing from thoughtful reflection they are going to end up in the tabloid press. You can never let down your guard.

CHAPTER 19

The Letters

A BOY IN Granada writes a letter to his father who has just been stationed in Madrid. Every word is resounding affirmation and proof that everything is fine, that he is studying and respectful with his schoolteachers, that he has cleaned his room and he hasn't diverted his siblings toward a path of domestic rebellion. The boy strives to write without any mistakes, with clear lettering and clean paper. There is no better justification than neat calligraphy for the presents being requested from a parent, with the quiver of innocence and the very well-aimed human instinct in the use of long-distance blackmail, the emotions of the holiday season.

Christmas is upon us. Snow virtually falls across the words in the letter. In the returning paternal luggage there will without a doubt be a space reserved for the objects listed with a steady hand, without deletions and practically wrapped already—as if it were gift-wrapping paper—by the diligent arrangement of the letters. The letter will arrive at its destination and then the days will pass slowly, the father will return to Granada. The boy will grow, become a man, and his life will lead him to the lovely, busy, melancholy winters of Madrid. In the life of a boy become a man, hardly anything is definitive, but there are many things that persist. Objects are a carousel. They disappear and then they return to you like Christmas in the almanac.

The man visits his parents in Granada and finds, when searching through family storage boxes, the letter that he wrote when he was a boy. He is not impressed that his father kept it. Nor is he surprised by the contents, which read like a naive catalog of phrases and predictable petitions. But he is moved when he sees on the front of the envelope the same street, the same number, the same flat, the same address that he now inhabits in Madrid. This tale is good enough to be fiction. Real life is never so perfect. There is usually some broken piece. For example, it is not exactly the same flat number. But it is the same street, and we are ensnared by the random assurance of human existence and its connection to objects.

We are always the recipients of saved objects and letters penned in childish hand. A child's letter presumes an appointment with its own future. We must respect and defend the folds of the past in order to discover our way to the future. The present obscures negotiation with time and with our past. Memories, the things that we keep and save, are knots of security in the cord that sustains our history, testimony that permits us to return to a time that no longer exists, because time is accustomed to changing address and disappearing forever if we don't snatch some personal object.

I have saved two letters I wrote as a boy. In one, my city, Granada, has taken refuge from the suffocation of construction. The other letter contains the sea. The gifts that I requested from my father when he was working in Madrid speak to me of the trees along the Paseo del Salón, the sports fields at my school, and the Sunday afternoon movies when the cowboys and Indians faced off. Living in the other letter are the youthful summers in Puerto de Motril, the endless siestas, fishing boats, and soccer matches broadcast on the radio. The words suddenly take on the form of a hook, a fishing rod, and a late afternoon on the porch with an adventure novel. Life is fused with these objects and protects us against their disappearance.

My wife saw me come home today carrying a field hockey stick and a shopping bag in which she soon discovered workout clothes, a collection of toy soldiers and a novel by Enid Blyton. But what is this, she asked. Nothing, I've just been out shopping in answer to a letter that I wrote to myself a long time ago. You are crazy, she said. My love, I said, I am crazy for you.

CHAPTER 20

Alberti's Tie

CLOSETS ARE THE hotels of time. The falsely familiar air of clocks, with their superficial discipline but internal disobedience, becomes an avowal of utter strangeness when we find ourselves in the closet with time. We like to think that the years roll along across a quiet world – the world is not quiet, and then things show up a size too big, with a missing button, with one too many springtimes of wear.

Before the days when Spanish youth had too much money, children used to inherit their wardrobes. I inherited mine from my mother's brother. The winters and the summers adapted themselves to my body in a decent fashion. My clothes needed minimal darning, a bit of hemming, a little patching on the seat of the trousers. That doesn't happen anymore. Youth now has too much of everything, including youth, and we feel ourselves children even after we have exceeded the seams of adulthood. Children are the majority now and they buy their clothes with credit cards in big department stores.

As an adult, I have been given many gifts of clothes for birthdays and saint's days. But in terms of inheriting, really inheriting, I have only a tie from Rafael Alberti. Closets are full of surprises. Perhaps one day that long-lost coat will appear. But in this moment, I am only wearing my eyes, just as at the beginning of each summer I wear Rafael's tie. It spends the rest of the year hidden, having taken off, flying like a bird from perch to perch, until it finds a nest of shadows. In the month of June, as I am searching for shirts still good from last summer, the tie appears with its thousand striking colors, its gaudy impertinence, its melancholy joy in living. Summer returns to the world much as an exile to his homeland. The joy is great, but the absence is great as well. The excess vitality of summer, with its red-hot thermometers, tries to compensate for all that has been lost, that which can never come back. The Caribbean, the jungle, permeate that tie given to me by Rafael, the exile who returned to Spain in 1977 sporting suit jackets and stentorian locks.

Many people live with the sole intention of never making a mistake. They may die without doing any wrong, but also without doing anything right. Professors intone that Alberti was a tumultuous poet, irregular, excessive. But he also created poems fundamental to the history of Spanish literature. A bad wedding doesn't deny the capacity to love, even if the wedding is as ponderous as a bronze statue next to the train station in the Puerto de Santa María. Rafael flew like he was a tie full of birds amidst the colors and the embraces, traveling from hotel to hotel, closet to closet, bearing the baggage of the exile, forged out of loss and pure vitality. When the absences became too heavy, he didn't put a noose to his neck, he preferred his tie amid the heaviest seas.

He gave his tie to me one day in August, after a visit to the Barranco de Víznar. It was made of Italian silk, but more importantly it was an item of clothing used by someone beloved, and I felt that I had inherited it just like my Uncle Quico's coats. Rafael gave many gifts; his currency was generosity. He even stepped down from his glorious exile's pedestal to share friendship with young apprentice poets. He dressed as an imprudent elder in a nation filling up with excessively sensible youth who have already perfectly measured and cut their futures as if they were navy-blue executive suits.

Rafael admired the world and its cuisines, just as he admired women and poetry. He wasn't sectarian, he read everything. He would recite a Renaissance sonnet or a vanguard poem, from Jorge Manrique to verses by Baudelaire. He moved from public multitudes to the solitude of his Princess Street apartment, a bohemian space always scattered with shirts and ties on every chair. To sit, you'd have to put out a fire or cross a jungle. Rafael's tie is like a summer, and one that doesn't end with the fall. It flies from perch to perch, disappearing before the cold arrives and returning each time the world dares to place itself in the hands of the sun.

CHAPTER 21

The Coasters

THE WORLD IS very much like an uneasy sleep. That's why we may often feel condemned to a vacuum, to discomfort and strangeness, and why occasionally we become monsters. After an uneasy sleep, Gregor Samsa, the protagonist of Kafka's *The Metamorphosis*, woke to find he had been transformed into a horrible insect. I've frequently transformed myself into a wine glass from the previous evening, a dirty glass abandoned on top of the table. It's not some human instinct or deep terror that causes these transformations. It is a vacuum. It would be gratifying to convince ourselves that the vacuum is created by some subjective essence, but that would require us to accept the existence of hell. The truth is that there are no good or bad essences, only history, and the choice to make oneself and unmake oneself out of nothingness. All that remains is the aftertaste.

That is what Antoine de Roquentin, the protagonist of Sartre's novel *Nausea*, discovered in the portrait gallery of the Bouville Museum. There the great fathers of the homeland, forgers of the city and its morals, posed in their prideful glory, but in their eyes glowed a yearning for concrete reality. Even this, however, was just an exercise in appearances, of ambition denied by history. Olivier Blévigne, a compact politician and the author of *The Duty to Punish*, was really a louse, a Mr. Nobody who used elevator shoes to reach the height of his speeches.

The search for solid worlds usually condemns us to alienation. But, believe me, there are rare moments of abundance, moments of both being and acting, that make us feel we are part of reality, fused in a cycle of natural existence superior to our helplessness. At times I have been fortunate enough to live those moments, and almost all of them I owe to the liquid world of light and bars.

Granada and Madrid are cities defined by their autumn skies. When the afternoon light fades into deep purples and violets, with timid streaks of clear gold and narrative intuitions that mix red and black, the two cities justify themselves to themselves. A serenity falls over them, a lyrical tranquility, over the hills, the rivers, the noble buildings and the plazas. Even the ugly office buildings along the modern streets rush to take advantage of this opportunity for beauty, and the walker feels a strange attraction, he is convinced by reality, he forms part of the world. He walks like a legitimate being in the light, a truth that is occupying its rightful place.

I confess that I have felt the same sensation of life in its rightful place, of reality perfectly situated, in some bars. I'm grateful of course for the familiar bars, those same old bars, in which the hours recognize us as if we were in our own home. The joy of the drink and the company, the routines of choice, the companionable countenances; all are less important than the diffuse sensation of belonging. The city is transformed into a personal reality. The vacuum moves away from us and disappears behind the bottles and glasses.

But I appreciate even more the surprises in the bars in unfamiliar cities, because they provide the same support as the autumn light, and the sensation of belonging is broader, more generous, until it becomes a form of intimacy in an alien world. Discovering a good bar means wanting to return, feeling part of a way of life, submerging yourself in the intimate joy of repetitions.

I've kept some of the coasters from my favorite bars and I enjoy finding them around the house. They appear between the pages of books, in corners of the shelves, like mementos of refuge and an invitation to return. A bar can be a city. On cold or rainy afternoons, in evenings of heat and humidity, with the weariness of the miles and uncertainties, with the impatience of available skin or the pulse of an unhappy heart, bars have given me at times a place to land, including a sense of belonging. When I drink alone at home, I raise my glass to all the customers of my favorite bars. They have helped me to understand the world.

CHAPTER 22

The State of Things

OLMOS HOUSE. THE butcher shop and groceries. 1958. It is an almanac of the year I was born, a present from José Emilio Pacheco. I rise from the table where I am writing and I look for December 4. A Thursday, Saint Barbara's Day. José Emilio says that writers born in December spend half the year seeming older than they are on the jacket flap of their books. Yes, being born in December can cause some misunderstandings. I look at the plastic figure of King Melchior who is currently resting on a shelf in the hallway. In a family with six kids, it wasn't a good idea to buy ceramic figurines. I grew up in a house in which everything got broken. Maybe that's why I have developed the habit of keeping everything as I grow older. The camel is long-legged, with bulging eyes and a poorly balanced hump, but the King holds up his scepter majestically and preserves under his faded blanket the treasure of a stable and closed world.

My father used to hide a saw underneath his heavy sweater when we went to the mountains to gather moss and cut down a small pine tree. That's how things were then. I have kept the saw in my toolbox, though the custom of taking nature into our own hands has now disappeared. That perfect world in which my father was able to fool the forest rangers has also disappeared. I am in great part to blame. Perfection disappears when you make a point of asking. Things are in their proper places, like the streets that lead to the school. The sky is like a blue sheet of paper, the stars are cardboard cutouts, the flour and the snow are white against the moss and the Three Kings cross a river of silver on a bridge made of cork. They proceed slowly toward those first questions. "Is he human or is he God?" "Do you want a cigarette?" my neighborhood friends asked me, with a Zippo lighter in hand. It was fascinating to see how they popped open the lid with a swipe of the hand against their jeans and how the flame disappeared with the same movement in reverse. It didn't take me long to start smoking, and it didn't take me long to buy my own Zippo, which I now have saved in one of my desk drawers. With its flame I burned away those many mornings at church, patriotic hymns, chores and the little packets of pastries that conventional families in my city would always take along on a visit.

Other things I didn't burn. I framed a betting slip. It was October 28, 1973; the debut of Cruyff in Barcelona and the Granada Soccer Club was visiting at Nou Camp stadium there. My team showed up without pastries and lost four to zero. Even the bad dates become nostalgic as the years go by. That's why I framed the betting slip, so it wouldn't get lost even though Granada had lost. Later I learned that other, worse things had happened on that same day. A few hours before the game, Solé Barbara, a historic communist lawyer, was arrested. It's a good thing that on the wall, right next to the betting slip, I also have a framed telegram from Dámaso Alonso to Rafael Alberti. It is addressed to the headquarters of the Communist Party, 8 calle Peligros: "Welcome, call me when you have a moment so I can come see you... Tlph. 2592337. Big hug." Rafael had just returned to Spain after a long exile. The dictatorship was ending. Friends were getting together again.

I have saved a drawing Juan Vida sketched on a paper tablecloth. It is a caricature of Armando, the waiter in the San Remo restaurant. I share with him the care of my liver. I save photos of my friends, surrounded by our old flags and empty glasses. I save many hours of wonder in this collection of greetings and farewells that is a library. And I save the receipt from the hotel where I spent the first night with the love of my life. I also save a picture of my son Mauro at the entrance to the zoo. I save a sheet of paper folded like a greeting card. My daughters Irene and Elisa painted a red heart on it for the best father in the world. They exaggerate because it's a birthday card. With a steady hand, the little girl writes the date, December 4.

I lost the love letters that my mother wrote to my father on blue paper in the exquisite handwriting taught by the nuns in Catholic schools. Those letters disappeared during a move, but I'm not sure whether it was my bad memory or because someone else threw them away to hurt me. Sometimes the things we lose are more present than the things we keep. Other times, not.

Amador, the Fernando León de Aranoa movie about immigration, awoke in me the desire to reread Steinbeck's *The Grapes of Wrath*. Social dramas and financial speculation anguish humans who are obliged to separate themselves from their things and learn to live with the hostility of a strange new world. The farmers of Oklahoma, condemned by drought and the banks, immigrated to California. They had to choose carefully which things they would take with them and which things they would lose forever. In each look, in each silence, there is strangeness and loss. Against the so-called creative destruction of capitalism, metaphors and mementos preserve free will, love of life, and respect for the past we embody. That life and death come to us doesn't mean that they should roll over us. To look to the future is to leave our heirs a sense of place, instead of a wilderness.

Fernando's movie led me to *The Grapes of Wrath* and Steinbeck to my mother's letters. Their absence led me this morning to go through one more time some of my mementos, touching each of them one by one; an act of rebellion, a form of resistance.

Translator's note

THE ORIGINAL SPANISH book *Una forma de resistencia* was published in May 2012 in Spain by Alfaguara, and includes more than fifty essays. In publishing this English-language edition, I selected twenty-two of them: those that had the most international—even universal—interest, and which required no detailed knowledge of Luis García Montero's work or of Spain. The essays that are not featured here are also very good and I strongly encourage those with a particular interest in Spain and a knowledge of Spanish to buy the Spanish-language edition. It's available as a Kindle eBook as well as in paperback.

I translated these essays into American English because, despite my happy residence in London for six years, I am American and I have never learned to speak "proper English," as my wonderful British husband will attest.

While this translation and whatever imperfections it may contain are all mine, I would like to thank my brilliant young bilingual British editor Ellie Robins, who does speak proper English as well as very proper Spanish. This book is so much better thanks to her efforts.

As a journalist who worked for years in Spain and Latin America, I've long written in both languages and translated back and forth, but almost always for news or business purposes.

I first started translating Luis's poetry in the late 2000s when I was introduced to his work by friends in Spain. I thought it so brilliant that I wanted to share it with my non-Spanish-speaking family and close friends. Their rapturous enjoyment of these poems spurred me to consider whether there might be a broader audience for them in English. With zero expectations for success I sent a few translations to the editors at Words Without Borders, the non-profit online literary magazine dedicated to bringing great international poetry and fiction to broad English-language audiences. WWB editor Susan Harris was an instant fan of Luis's poetry and I will be forever grateful for her enthusiasm and encouragement. With kind support from Luis's Spanish publisher Alfaguara, my translations of his work have now appeared online on WWB and in print in *New European Poets*, an anthology published in 2008 by Graywolf Press.

I am grateful for and honored by Luis's generous and consistent backing for this first book-length translation project. I hope it inspires more translations of his writing for English-language audiences to enjoy.

About the Author

Luis García Montero (b. 1958) http://luisgarciamontero.com is one of Spain's most acclaimed and award-winning poets. He is a professor at the University of Granada and a founding member of a major poetic movement in Spain called "Poetry of Experience." In addition to poetry, García Montero's prolific output includes short stories, literary translations, novels, essays and political commentary.

Made in the USA
Charleston, SC
14 September 2015